YELLOW ARROW

Vol. X, No. 1
Spring 2025
Unfurl

Yellow Arrow Journal

Creative nonfiction, poetry, and cover art by writers and
artists identifying as women

Vol. X, No. 1
Spring 2025
Unfurl

Editor-in-Chief
Kapua Iao

Guest Editor
Sara J. Streeter

Creative Director
Alexa Laharty

UNFURL Editorial Team
Arrieonna Derricoatte, Jill Earl, Angela Firman, Barbara Frey,
Meg Gamble, Jacqueline Goldman, Gabby Granillo,
Siobhan McKenna, Melissa Nunez, Kait Quinn,
Leticia Priebe Rocha, and Emily Ross

Contributors
Storm Ainsely, Heather Brown Barrett, Michelle Bovée Stange,
Kellie D. Brown, Tricia Gates Brown, Carrie Aurelius Carlisle,
Brandy Bell Carter, Alexis F., Hillary Gonzalez, LuLu Grant,
Melanie Hyo-In Han, Kalehua Kim, Majiq Vu Mai, Mansi,
Sini Marcks, Mary McAfoose, Shannon McNicholas, Nia P.,
Emma Reyes, Lindsay B. Sears, Alyce Shu, Cat Speranzini,
Beverley Sylvester, Laura Taber, Bethany Tap, Jo Tyler,
and Jessica Zarrillo

YELLOW ARROW

PUBLISHING

PO Box 65185, Baltimore, MD 21209
info@yellowarrowpublishing.com

Yellow Arrow Journal - UNFURL
Copyright © 2025 by Yellow Arrow Publishing
All rights reserved.

ISBN (paperback): 978-1-967202-00-3
ISSN (print): 2688-3015
ISSN (online): 2688-3023

Cover art and design by Alexa Laharty (Instagram
@alexaelisabeth). Interior design by Yellow Arrow Publishing.
For more information, see yellowarrowpublishing.com.

*We prioritize the unique voice and
style of each of our authors.*

*Every writer has a story to tell and
every story is worth telling.*

Yellow Arrow Publishing

Fruit of the Spirit

Kellie D. Brown

The truest nature of a living thing
declares itself as it is plucked,
strained, smashed, scarred.

The lemon scraped for zest
unmasks its crisp, acidic gist;
the orange squeezed for juice
spills its sweet, sunny essence;
the coffee bean ground for brew
bares its dark, nutty marrow.

We are the same.
Drained, chafed, stripped, scavenged,
we submit to the great unveiling;
a betrayal, a benediction;
the glorious among the grotesque.

Table of Contents

Dear Readers,

Yellow Arrow Journal's Vol. X, No. 1, issue **UNFURL** is a tribute to our collective and individual transmutation. In this issue, you'll find rest and unrest, the never-ending journey to ourselves—and then back again. Each **UNFURL** piece explores someone's unique process of transformation, and when strung together, form a vibrant narrative about the Yellow Arrow community. I am honored to bear witness to stories that weave perspective and deep reflection into such strength. They remind me that community and imagination are powerful gifts we all have access to.

"Unfurl" means numerous, different, beautiful things to our 28 contributors, and each piece deserves to be encapsulated, starting with the opening poem of the issue, Kellie D. Brown's "Fruit of the Spirit," which contemplates how we, like a lemon or a coffee bean, come to "declare" our "truest nature." Then, in Beverley Sylvester's "Chrysalis" and Majiq Vu Mai's "The Metamorphosis," unfurl implies transformation, breaking free from the things that both protect us and hold us down.

Following these, Jo Tyler's "Anything," Nia P.'s "My Fig Tree Has Peaches," and Hillary Gonzalez's "On Hawks, Night Herons, and Softness," the narrators use the theme to reflect on the thrill of seeing (finding?) their true potential. Next, Shannon McNicholas' "Field of Sunflowers," Alexis F.'s "Sinner Sundays," Emma Reyes' "The Place Where I Live Most of the Time," and Brandy Bell Carter's "Oh, Honey" use unfurl to understand how certain relationships shaped each of them. We then become flies on the wall during defining moments, episodes, in Tricia Gates Brown's "Posed-for Nudes," and Heather Brown Barrett's "A Bone to Pick."

Picking up on relationships, Mansi's "In the Dark: Unbound, Unafraid" and Cat Speranzini's "I hope you have a daughter just like you," help us to recognize ourselves in our children and then through our parents, as in Lindsay B. Spears' "Sustenance," Michelle Bovée Stange's "My father's coat / my own coat," Storm Ainsely's "I listen to Gregory & the Hawk, Boats & Birds," Melanie Hyo-In Han's "An Apple as Apology," Bethany Tap's "Chartreuse is shaped like red," and LuLu Grant's "回家."

Eventually, our gaze shifts inward, with unfurl as confession in Carrie Aurelius Carlisle's "EIGHTH OF SEPTEMBER," Kalehua Kim's "There's a trick with a pen I'm learning to do," Sini Marcks' "EXHIBIT OF WOMEN AND AWE," Mary McAfoose's "Body as a river channel," Jessica Zarrillo's "It was pleasure, and I clung to it," and Laura Taber's "Unwrapping."

UNFURL ends poignantly with Alyce Shu's "The Pool," a journey through unfurling as boundless inspiration. *Yellow Arrow Journal* **UNFURL** is a remarkable, brave collection written by creatives who identify themselves as women, nonbinary, queer, disabled, autistic, and people of color, many who carry intersecting identities. I see **UNFURL** as an act of resistance in a moment when there is a push for the erasure of words such as "women," "immigrants," "community," and "gay." Instead of shrinking themselves down, the authors within these pages choose to be visible, to stretch out toward the sun with remarkable grace and courage.

Thank you, reader, for being a part of this issue by meandering through the included prose and poems. And thank you, contributors, for sharing your journey, yourselves, and your hearts. It's a tremendous privilege to walk alongside the living words of every included piece. Onward to joy.

In solidarity,

Sara J. Streeter 안혜숙

UNFURL

Chrysalis

Beverley Sylvester

The caterpillar liquefies before it becomes the butterfly but retains its memories. We don't know why. By we I mean science. By science I mean a map of time and inches. Once upon a time I thought my parents were made of silk and fire. Once upon a time I realized they were people. It is hard to learn the complications of personhood, to learn no one is perfect, to learn that before we can grow we must wrap ourselves into darkness and dissolve. People are messy like unformed caterpillar goo. People turn opinions into deals into stone monuments to tiny gods of right and wrong. People turn ideals into a game of checkers: straight lines, boxes, kings, winners. Gray is harder but truer. Maybe there aren't monsters in the dark, in the closet, under the bed. I think that darkness can live outside the monsters. I think the bogeyman is an influencer. I wish there were a ratio of pain and joy that equaled art. It's a fool's wish, and it is scared of grayness. Sometimes I cry without knowing why, and I don't know if that's better than walls of thick skin. I envy the cynics their simple perspective. I don't envy the cynics. Perhaps the world is uglier than when we were children. Caterpillar protein soup is ugly. But have you ever seen a butterfly?

The Metamorphosis

Majiq Vu Mai

I am seven. My father tucks me into bed the same way he always does. A kiss on a cheek, a hug, and the same little ritual, spoken like a spell. "Good night. Sleep tight . . ."

The firm clasp of two pinkies making a promise to each other. ". . . don't let the bedbugs bite."

✳✳✳✳

A simple park with a circular design, St. Mary's was situated just two blocks away from me and my partner's shared apartment in Baltimore. For me, the park was a sanctuary to release the intrusive thoughts that consumed my mind. My own mental, psychological escape.

My shepherd feist mix, Lorde, and I were on the last stretch of our midnight stroll when we came across a funny looking leaf. I felt compelled to step over it for whatever reason. Call it intuition, vibes, or just raw instinct. Just as I stuck out my foot to nudge it, the leaf gave a loud, frantic shrill. A bat! My eyes adjusted to its insignificant form on the pavement. It looked small and sad there, struggling under the park's dim lights. I considered moving it to avoid getting trampled by another walker but thought it best to leave creepy creature where creepy creatures lie. Lorde and I walked away, abandoning it in the darkness behind us. As I walked, I consulted Google on my phone, trying to make meaning out of this strange sign.

> "Bats often represent death in the sense of letting go of the old and bringing in the new. They are symbols of transition, of initiation, and the start of a new beginning."[1]

---

1 The quote is from pure-spirit.com/more-animal-symbolism/222-pure-spirit-minneapolis-st-paul-dog-training-and-international-all-species-animal-communication-bat.

An eerie feeling tickled the cherry red curls of my hair sitting on the back of my neck. I shrugged it off and continued walking. No use worrying over what hadn't come yet, even if a representation of change was at my feet.

The next morning, my partner asked me if I had time for a quick chat. I listened to them, sipping coffee at the edge of my bed. It wasn't until they finished and said the phrase three times that the message they shared sank in: we had bedbugs.

> "You must understand that every step listed below must be completed in order to achieve the desired result, which is 100% elimination of bedbugs from your apartment. Keep in mind that a SINGLE BEDBUG can go dormant for '2' years without feeding. Should you miss any step listed, you can and most likely will not achieve success in eliminating this problem."[2]

You never really know what you have in your home, what you've accumulated, until bedbugs infiltrate it and make you move everything. Tiny, pointless pests the size of a flat screw head, bedbugs love to snack on human flesh. They'll hide anywhere they can latch onto—your clothes, your baseboards, your spirit. A bedbug infestation can feel like a full-blown attack. Pest control tells you not to sleep in different rooms once you have them. Moving around will only help them spread. When my partner shared that we had these new neighbors in our home, I could feel my body disconnecting from my head and a foreboding sense settling in.

> "Empty ALL bureaus, end tables, coffee tables, nightstands, and closets. This includes all personal items and clothing."

Typically, my bedroom functioned as the ultimate shell for an introverted hermit like myself—an elusive cave tucked away

---

2 This and the four quotes that follow are from the bedbug preparation requirements letter the author's apartment received from Moran's Elite Termite and Pest Management Inc., on September 6, 2024.

from the prying eyes of the outside world, protecting the softest parts of me. My bedroom was so precious to me that I only shared it with my partner on occasion, when I felt like cuddling with another warm body to quell my desire for physical affection. With rose mauve walls lined with bold, manic art; it was my safe haven. My altar. My play space. My everything. My nightstand. Equipped with water, remotes, toothpicks, and a phone stand connecting me to the outside world. It allowed me to suffer in my bed for hours, while I spiraled during hypomanic episodes. My dark wood dresser. It sat cata-cornered by the window, a vertical accordion full of fabric and hidden seams. Sentimental T-shirts, party gear, an inconsistent array of panties and socks; I didn't realize I had so much clothing. My canary yellow cabinet. It burst with COVID tests and other medicinal supplements, a dependable portal that swallowed the aches and pains of my life. My favorite decor bowl, shaped like a gold bird's nest. It cradled my silver hoop earrings, an obsidian protection ring, and a brass ring engraved with bold letters that read "SLUT." I felt like a hermit crab forced out of its favorite shell; my exoskeleton vulnerable to the whims of a violent world. Every drawer emptied felt like a violent shake into the unknown. My little crab legs, exposed, as I was forced to empty out every cabinet and closet I found comfort hiding in.

> "You must put all clothing, bed linens, blankets, towels, and all other washables including curtains and drapes into large plastic bags."

I bundled up my plush pillows, duvet comforter, and sheer linen curtains; I threw them into big commercial dryers with the rest of my sheets, then into storage. My extra long stiletto nails snagged on every bit of fabric. The sensation felt like pulling out pointy, cartilage teeth. I couldn't separate my panties from my winter coats or my towels and getting dressed every morning in such a tight space felt like a rigged game designed to torture me. I kept running into corners I never knew existed. I mourned the pink-purple bruises scattered across my thighs. My bipolar disorder flared up. I found it hard to stay grounded, my mood swings stuck at a dangerous peak. I was left with the bare minimum to cover my nakedness, all my comfort stripped bare from my space for the full six weeks I was locked down. I lashed out at loved ones who tried to help me regulate and crowdfund as I struggled to manage the drastic fluctuations in my mood swings. Some of those loved ones eventually walked away. Bipolar disorder is not the easiest roommate to share a body with, and therapy wasn't a financial option at the time. All that patient love, wasted. All my shit, thrown into tightly sealed garbage bags and ugly plastic containers. All my shit, inaccessible and hard to reach, pushed into the center of my space. A mountain of my own shit, just staring at me.

> "Wash all items listed above in hot soapy water and then you MUST put them in a new plastic bag. If you use the same bag over again, you take the risk of re-infesting all the items you just washed. Make sure you throw away all bags that were used before items were washed."

"Have you seen my keys?" My partner crouched at the entrance of my bedroom, their slender brown hands cupped around their cute hips. "Didn't you set them on top of the bookshelf?" I replied as I stopped my compulsive fiddling. I put down the Lysol wipes and trash bags clenched in my hand. I always seemed to be holding them in my hands. "The bookshelf I just cleaned off. . . ?" Their words shrunk in their mouth, their unibrow wrinkled in concentration. We stood there for several seconds, just staring at each other, before adrenaline finally kicked in, and we decided to dig further.

We walked down our apartment's long corridor hallway, weaving through piles of miscellaneous junk shoved against the walls because of the turmoil. I whispered a quick prayer to

St. Anthony and slid my hands along every inch of the bookshelf that sat between the end of the long hallway and the entrance to the kitchen. My partner rifled through the stacks of old mail and legal documents that cluttered our glass kitchen table thinking they may have been put there. We performed a thorough military sweep of the entire apartment. We couldn't find the keys anywhere.

"Did you put them in one of your pants pockets?" I asked. "I must have . . ." my partner replied. Our eyes traveled to the big, tightly sealed blue bags filled with already dried and clean laundry. We considered the risks and weighed the options. They needed those keys. They couldn't go to work without them. One by one, my partner opened every sealed bag of laundry, rummaging through clothes that I had spent hours washing and drying. I sulked into the kitchen, grabbing a set of new garbage bags, a new set of bitter tears streaming down my face.

> "All people and pets must be out of the apartment at
> time of service and 4 hours after service is completed."

****

I felt like a wandering spirit, walking into my apartment after the final fumigation. My footsteps echoed as I walked through the mountains of garbage bags still surrounding me like a baby blue sea. I walked toward the entrance of my bedroom. I took a deep breath and stepped inside. My imagination ricocheted off the walls, echoing the visions I had spent weeks conjuring in my mind as we waited for pest control to complete the fumigation process. Instead of being centered against the main wall, my bed would be pushed up close to my pretty plant-filled window, so that I could get more fresh air and easily absorb the sun. A new writing desk would be tucked away in the makeshift study nook that was once my closet, while my clothes hung free on an open wardrobe rack for more range and accessibility. And my future stripper pole would sit at the center of it all, breaking the space in-between.

I saw myself hanging upside down on the pole, held up by my strong, thick thighs. I saw myself spinning, lost in the darkness, breaking past the branches on the window that threatened to poke out my eyes. I saw myself resting afterward on the floor of my bedroom, catching my breath. *Take your time. Take your time.* All this time, and the best thing I could do, the only thing I could really do, was take my time. When I couldn't control the outcome, I would take my time. When I couldn't breathe in between heavy loads of laundry and furniture, I would take my time. When my body felt like fire, consumed by the livid flareups of a mood disorder that burns its own wick at an unsustainable pace, all I could do was take my time.

I thought about that funny leaf, the bat, that I saw before the bedbug catastrophe. A flying creature caught on the ground, struggling to see beyond tiny limbs stretched out in front of it. What could small flying creatures like us do after a life shaking fall like that, but take our time? *A symbol of transition and initiation.* I wondered what I looked like now, after everything.

Hopefully, transformed and free.

Anything

Jo Tyler

When I was small, you told me
I could be anything.
It wasn't true, but it was good of you
to say, and help me believe
for a moment, so the world would
feel like windows and doors unlocked,
thrown open to strange vistas
and mysteries, so that I would
waltz across thresholds, fearless
and unfettered. And I did. And I fell
up into the sky, in love with starlings
and clouds, swifts and soft rain.

When I was a youth, the guidance
counselor told me I shouldn't
want to be a psychiatrist
because I would have to learn
Latin, and my English teacher
Mr. Hamilton declared that I was not
college material. *What kind then,*
I worried, *what kind of material
am I?* And you said, *You are soft
velvets and vibrant silks. That man
is only a man behind a curtain.
Pay attention to me: You can
be anything.* It still wasn't true,
but still so good of you
to say, and to help me believe it
in the face of my education
about "No."

And in all of the time
I was doing what I believed
I should do, so that later
I could be anything,
I told you this was
the anything that I wanted
to be. It wasn't true.
I was only picking up shiny
objects that crossed my path,
tokens that gave me
access to narrow doors
into the world of men
making machines, messes,
and money, because in an odd
twist of timing, it became
the right thing to let a woman
advance—a little, not too much,
just enough; a Goldilocks
moment of compromise
where I gazed out the closed
windows from inside, upstairs,
dreaming of escaping into sky.

And now, I am old,
and you are gone,
and the men are still
in charge from behind
the curtain, but they have
decided I don't matter
anymore, and I can go ahead
and be a poet and write
in questionable rhythm
to the percussion and strings
that have been playing

in my heart and head
this whole time.
And when my pen
presses on paper,
I can be anything.

My Fig Tree Has Peaches

Nia P.

I daydream often.
One minute I'm listening to soul,
The next I'm dancing in blue
Pointe ballet shoes.
The spotlight pours and gratefully
There's no crowd,
No standing ovation.
I'm thinner here, twirling, elegant.
I'm named Grace,
Not Heavy-Footed,
As my grandmother has called me.

I'm a day spent scrubbing
Porcelain plates,
Hands slicked in suds.
I'm far away,
Amongst wildflowers.
I point them out, naming each:
Lavender lupines, sunset paintbrushes,
Winter avalanche lilies.

There I am, shooting film,
Sipping rich river water.
I've never been here.
Yet, I'm sure it cures a curse
Like the one I call beautiful.
Already, my skin feels broken in,
Warm like honey, spread with delight.

In the morning, I wake up to white walls,
A place where I can paint in the lines.
In a world where I'm worthy,
The grass is always green,
I'm all that I ever could be;
Everything to some
And nothing to me.
But never let me go.

On Hawks, Night Herons, and Softness
Hillary Gonzalez

What will I do until spring returns?

I keep taking short walks

down to the bridge, where the Jones Falls runs lazily,

to where the Yellow-Crowned Night Herons

lovingly build their homes

in the spring and summer months,

their nest balancing precariously over the water.

I miss the awkward long necks of their young

and the bright red of the adults' eyes watching me.

The Red-Shouldered Hawks have moved on,

and I wonder if the new generation will return

to the sycamore tree in front of my house

to raise new young, shrieking from

the tree canopy, momentarily silencing the forest.

I am learning how to make my soft belly softer.

I remind myself that even the hawk,

with her sharp beak and talons,

is covered in soft feathers.

I am learning that my gentle nature

is my greatest strength.

The world around me keeps knocking

on the sheltered reservoir of my heart,

trying to get in, trying to dilute it,

trying to poison it against my nature.

Let me be soft awhile longer.

Let me share this way of being with others.

A robin calls in the distance, high and bright

and reminiscent of warmer months.

Once, long ago, I spurned my soft nature.

There were others who tore and ripped at it,

convinced me I should harden

and become a creature, unrecognizable

even to myself.

But, I am not that creature.

I am becoming something more.

Something others might see and know.

When spring arrives, dressed in

luminescent forsythia and daffodils,

I think she will smile on how I, too, have changed.

Field Of Sunflowers

Shannon McNicholas

"Your heart needs new parts," Dad says, "they'll fix you."
I imagine the vibrance you'll emanate when you heal.

Pelted with rain, sunflowers tip toward the ground.
In minutes, they unfurl, even more open and alive than before.

Your family flies from Texas, California, West Virginia,
to hold your hand as you tip toward the ground.

Colossal, shining yellow light above and below. Impossible to ignore.
Stems and greens, 12-foot-tall, with dense blooms, 18-inch-diameter.

In weeks, in months, you will form a scar, slow
and painful at first; then you, more alive than before.

A sunflower's germination and return to earth takes place over
8 months, blooming vibrantly when established in the correct season.

Sinner Sundays

Alexis F.

the last Sunday of summer,
sweat slid down her face
faster than a cloud pouring
floods from its womb.

her lips,
born from saltwater
and Carolina taffy,
press themselves on a girl
with hands she likes holding.

the two walking and skipping
behind curtains of the river's
mouth, feeling stiff winds
pant on their hair.

they play tag,
a game known through
currency of fertile hands.

and grandma,
hands heavier than the weight
of this sunshine,
watches from the screen door
lips of two girls
weaving into the other,
back and forth.

and grandma
grabs Bible and belt,
becomes holder of the heaviest
lightning.
her frazzled leather-rope
strikes the girl's back,

puddling her white shirt
into red sea.

The Place Where I Live Most of the Time
Emma Reyes

I have learned to take breaths between stretches
and to continue asking: how do giraffes sleep?

Legs tucked between themselves—folding
or simply collapsing the way

a house bouquet knows to wither.
I don't know why it makes me sad.

On a walk, Magnolia feathers on the ground
resemble bone. They remember the small

of a shoulder blade, of what it is to have been
alive and to have died.

Is there a way to convince you these are all the ways
I know how to miss you?

Turning everything into a question and bullet points,
everything into your favorite natural disaster—avalanche

of light—avalanche of something that makes rainbows
glow the way they do.

I think I love you the way—
yes, yes, I love you the way

I love how animals do not know
what August is or that snow is snow.

Two white doves become just one beam of light,
and for some reason, that makes them less pure.

You throw away the checks your mom sends you
and text her *thank you* like you use them.

One day you say you're scared of dying
because you haven't slow danced enough.

You are my favorite day of the week.
Your hands are softer than mine.

On the beach under a Pink Moon, everything but you
is mist. Your body, the only real thing I want to touch,

the only thing I can. I give you a shell.
It ends up carrying a crab, and we're here again tomorrow.

Two of my dad's best friends died,
and he told me in passing.

Sergio loved Billy Joel, and Manny
FaceTimed me two months ago.

Last night, someone drove by my house at 4 a.m.
blasting "Don't Stop 'Til You Get Enough"

in a distant echo or fog or winter air.
When a wound disappears, I miss that, too.

You and I are snow leopards. We are
sacred versions of tenderness.

You know how to take off my clothes.

Posed-for Nudes

Tricia Gates Brown

When I knew I was leaving you, I burned
the evidence: the manila envelope of nudes
you'd taken of me, developed in a makeshift
darkroom in our basement, a space
haunted with boxed memories and mold.

What rooms had I posed in?
I cannot recall. In that house where
I inch-by-inched up shag carpet
in green and gold. Painted the walls
with half-can remnants found in our

decrepit garage—exhuming
beauty from stale tableaus. I now wish
I could see those photos. Look into the eyes
of that girl, with her minute breasts
and velvet, equine hips—to catch sight

of the seduction; what it would teach
of duplicity. Yet that is why they could not
exist—their openness, like fecund seeds,
captured in grainy black-and-white, fodder
for extortion. When I told you I had destroyed

the photos, you cried. My taking away
those images, a more profound grief
than my taking away our daughter. You
mourned the loss of that nude girl with lurid
eyes replaced by the marble-cold gaze of a woman,

learning to pose only for herself.

A Bone to Pick

Heather Brown Barrett

Your best friend's older brother preys over you at the Presbyterian Church playground, where you swing and sing Amy Grant songs. His pals straddle bicycles as he shouts that you better cuss, better say what he says, or he'll beat you up, punch you in the face, he'll "Punch your ugly, yellow teeth right out your mouth!" Imagine, tiny doves released from the den of a mouth, like an illusionist's sleight of hand. How you cower like a frightened bird, wings hugging body as the bully threatens to rape you, when you don't even know what that means. So you squawk and squawk and squawk every expletive he barks and bids you parrot, jerking your head back the way a heron does to swallow a herring. His goons howl like jackals, like they've snared fresh meat, like their clamor can claw through skin, through sinew and muscle, can tussle for the beating organ in your nine-year-old chest. Little bird, a heart can be a beat or beast, slamming within a ribcage; selfless and selfish, two sides of the same tender token.

A boy from the entourage hollers, "Hey, Sunshine, close that yellow mouth! The light's blinding me!" Sunshine, the sarcastic moniker christened to you by fellow children, a nickname to loathe. Your best friend sobs from the slide. Her brother stalks you to the church parking lot, shoves you for trying to leave, shoves so hard your spine might splinter. He shoves so hard you land on hands and knees. He growls in your ear, "Better not tell, bitch. Say something, and I'll hurt you." This isn't the first time, and won't be the last, that you're a target for cruelty and conquest. Little bird, children know nothing of amelogenesis imperfecta: a genetic condition that weakens and discolors teeth, that imbues a body with the ability to carry light. You stand and steel your backbone, ignore the sting of scraped knees and palms and the welling of scarlet blood on both. You erase fear from your face—

an attempt to look unruffled. Your captor finally says, "This is stupid. Let's go." He stomps to his bicycle, and the pack of boys pedals off, moaning and whooping with exaggerated pitch as they bike down the pine-lined street. You head home, voice lodged like a fishbone in your throat—you will not tell your mother.

Little sparrow, free the song from silence. Your heart is heavy, but mercy weighs less than hatred. Release your rage, let it scatter from your open mouth like sunlight through the shadow of memory, like tiny golden doves soaring, searching for an olive branch.

Oh, Honey
Brandy Bell Carter

I read about the roots of trees—
How the forest holds itself up,
Holds itself together.

Held up by
Woods full of women:
Teachers, mentors, sisters, friends.
When storms strike,
My branches may sway,
Yet they have come to link their limbs around me
To say, "Oh, Honey!"
A comfort straight from their heartwood.

Compassion wears the everyday clothes
Of a voice tinged in Appalachia,
Raspy from a pack a day,
Or the sentences on a page.
I consume another daughter's tale, and it's
My story, too.
Their words and wombs and wounds
Have carried me so far.

Today I am a mature oak
Spreading out rooted tendrils and twigs to steady
Saplings growing in my shade.

Oh, Honey,
Don't apologize
For needing
For taking up space
For weeping or wanting
For asking all the hard questions.

All I can offer is the refrain I learned as a girl:
Oh, Honey,
Oh, Honey,
Oh, Honey.
I'm here.

In the Dark: Unbound, Unafraid
Mansi

Her cries cut through the autumn night like shattered glass. I sit, crumpled at the bottom of our carpeted stairs, 10 feet from her bedroom door, my forehead pressed against my knees, sobbing, gasping for breath. The cold hardwood floor makes its presence felt through my thin pajamas, and somewhere in the distance the Caltrain horn holds the promise of escape. My husband stands guard at her door, his shadow stretching down the hallway like a barrier between us. I haven't slept, eaten, or felt like myself in weeks; questioning everything I was, am, and becoming.

I will myself to stay still. Just five more minutes. That's what the books say, what the pediatrician suggests, what every friend who has "figured it out" tells us. But her cries aren't fading. They aren't learning. They are breaking with the intensity of a raging volcano. And something inside me cracks with them. Through my tears, I watch my husband's silhouette—the weary slope of his shoulders, the way his teeth clench and unclench. He doesn't look at the ghost of the woman he once knew, sitting sadly beside him. His wife, the woman who once laughed at dinner parties, who fell asleep in his arms instead of curled around a nursing baby. The person he has spent the past 13 years loving. Where has she gone? He isn't cruel, just desperate to believe that a different way exists, where we can all get what we need: sleep, touch. Reassurance that we are not failing as a couple or as parents. Other Indian couples we know have seemingly mastered the sleep transition. Their babies sleep in separate rooms, their traditionally arranged marriages sail smoothly, and their lives keep turning. Why isn't it easy for us?

Her cries continue to fill the house, and I know what she needs most. I press my palms against my ears, but her shrieks burrow deeper. They vibrate in my chest, echo in my bones, and stir something ancient and unnamed. A voice I didn't know I had rose from the deep—raw, undeniable, primal—unfurling like a fern after rain, reaching toward something old and true. The woman who has spent decades folding herself smaller, making herself fit, begins to stretch toward air.

I stand up.

✶✶✶✶

After my daughter was first born, depression slipped into my bones like winter air through cracked windows, unnoticed at first, then impossible to shut out. Some mornings, I sat on the kitchen floor staring at unwashed dishes, unable to remember when I had last spoken in full sentences. The days blurred together in an endless cycle of vigilance: reading every food label, carrying an EpiPen, preparing meals from scratch that wouldn't trigger her 32 allergies. The simple act of leaving the house became an exercise in strategic planning. Birthday parties meant packing everything separately: cupcakes, snacks, drinks. Wipes. Lots of wipes. Each gathering outside our house was a reminder that we lived in a world that wasn't built for her needs.

"This is too much," my mother muttered one afternoon, watching me scrub the blender twice before making my daughter's food. "In our time, children ate what we gave them." She said it so casually, as if survival were a matter of preference. Did she not realize (or care) that her granddaughter could die from an anaphylactic reaction?

Later that same night on FaceTime, my mother-in-law added fuel to the fire while talking to my husband. "She had her too late, that's why. Now the child is too precious." Both of their words hung in the air like smoke, seeping into every corner of my already clouded mind. The weight of their judgment pressed against me like a physical thing. Don't nurse her at night. Don't carry her everywhere. Don't co-sleep. Don't skip the ear-piercing ceremony at three months. Don't let her eat meat. Don't give her cold drinks when she's sick. Don't bathe her in the evening.

Each "don't" felt like another brick in a wall I was desperately trying to break down. At my lowest point, I found myself staring at a bottle of ibuprofen, wondering how much it would take to make everything stop. But even then, even at my darkest, my body knew better than my mind. It rejected the escape, choosing instead to keep fighting, keep protecting, keep loving.

****

My legs are steady as I cross the hallway. My husband starts to protest but stops when he sees my face. This isn't the same woman who has spent years trying to please everyone. This isn't the woman who tried to please the world—her parents, his parents, every unspoken rule. This isn't his wife, hollowed by exhaustion, trying to be a perfect mother. This is someone else, someone new.

"Move!"

He does.

I open the door. I pick her up. We cry. All three of us engulfed in a hug.

Each decision afterward shows the change in my trajectory. We skip the ear-piercing ceremony until she is ready at nine years old. I learn to make potstickers alongside dal. When she is sick, I give her Popsicles and pho—things that comfort her but defy tradition. Each choice feels like I am removing another layer of expectations, revealing something truer underneath.

Now, a decade later, I watch my daughter navigating the world with a confidence I've never had. Her favorite foods are a map of cultures: Vietnamese, Mexican, Japanese, Indian. She moves effortlessly between worlds that I once thought had to remain separate. Sometimes, watching her navigate this freedom, I feel a flutter of uncertainty. Have I built her a bridge or have I untethered her completely?

During Diwali, when she prefers 85% dark chocolate truffles to traditional sweets or stumbles over basic Hindi phrases that my mother-in-law throws at her, I wonder if I've given her too much space to grow in her own direction. But then I see how she holds both worlds—lighting diyas with careful reverence, then participating in the Mandarin cultural presentation at school, singing songs I don't understand—I realize that roots can stretch without breaking. Recently, we started to keep a notebook together. When words feel too big for our voices, we write them down. No discussion is needed, just an honest exchange. Last night, she wrote, "Sometimes I feel different from everyone else. Is that bad?" I sat with the weight of those words, remembering that night at the stairs, remembering every small act of rebellion that followed. I wrote back, "Different isn't wrong. Different is brave."

That night long ago, I had picked her up and broken the rules. And now, as she stands on the precipice of teendom, she is writing her own. As I watch her move through the world—bold, joyful, independent, entirely herself—I understand what that moment really meant. In breaking from conformity, obligation, duty, and unquestioned rules on how to parent, I wasn't destroying something precious. I was making space for her to plant roots in her own soil—to evolve into something uniquely hers.

I hope you have a daughter just like you
Cat Speranzini

with steely eyes that harden like rocks,
partially covered in a thick coat of moss.
A forest in and of herself, growing
despite her doubts. Stubborn as a bull
and swift as a fox. Shades of red
tumbling, cascading, becoming soft
down the base of her neck.
All split ends and gap teeth.
A mischievous smirk, a playful leap
from grassy banks to jagged edges.
Hard to love or precious?
I hope you have a daughter just like you,
you say the syllables as a threat.
But, she's on the ground collecting ants,
moving them from puddle to pavement.
"So they don't drown," she says, brows fiercely set.
And I contemplate if it's a curse:
being brave enough to protect
those who will never understand
the kindness.

Sustenance

Lindsay B. Sears

After I'd left, my mom
would think of me
as the bumblebee
searching for sweetness within
the cowslip and the cranesbill
she let run rampant
in the yard. I think
gathering me in this way,
among her favorite colors
and living things,
may have sustained
the work of smiling
and the heat necessary
to brood.

On anniversary days,
thoughts of my mom
bloom on the lips of aunties
and sisters and friends.
And I flit about
from house to house
and collect the pieces
of her that can carry me
through the fall.

My father's coat / my own coat
Michelle Bovée Stange

After my father died I wove myself a thick cocoon of grief, as if the world, a waiting shark, would not notice me if I sat still and quiet in my blanket of memories. As if it would bow gracefully and wait for me to make the first move when I was good and damn well ready to emerge from my spent chrysalis. Only life does not step back; it tugs at hems and loose threads until whole great bare patches emerge, raw and aching, and no matter how firmly I wrapped myself there were always empty grumbling stomachs, broken faucets drip-drip-dropping water, faulty batteries in need of replacements, and balmy summer evenings to enjoy outside. There was also a toddler, a lighthouse glowing bright, who pulled me from my snug hideaway to join in his daily dramas and delights, only to send me running back for my cocoon of remembering when I felt that he was no longer the baby his grandfather knew.

Eventually the edges of the cocoon became so frayed and tattered that I could not cover the parts of me that had emerged since the past ended and the future began. The back-and-forth between the land of the living, with the parabolas of everyday and the wilderness of growing up, and the land of memory, where the moths of time were busy chewing holes, was unsustainable. And I saw that perhaps I had been letting my own seams fray for a long time, so certain that my father would always be puttering around and ready to patch me up with kind words and wry perspective. One night I decided on a new project. I wrote a list of all my father's traits, the ones I had relied on and admired and missed terribly; the ones that I needed to keep and the ones I needed my son to know. There in the darkness, I wove them together into a brilliant coat that I could slip into in the morning to cover the gaps in my own fabric until the threads merged. Life will pull and snag and snarl, edges will wear, but I have the pattern here in my fingertips. It was always mine, anyway.

I listen to Gregory & the Hawk,
Boats & Birds

Storm Ainsely

It was me who told my sister our parents were getting a divorce &
Dad didn't know yet. She was my copilot of a U-Haul. We were helping
a friend, driving across the state where it all began:
                                                My name. My lip scars. When
even the dog started anxiety-licking her paws like we kids bite our nails.
My first job to support the family—bankruptcy loomed. Dad was
already a state ahead of us & we were all stuck in the house For Sale.
                        Because we'd all bought it. The promise of staying
put. We thought we were finally growing roots.
        We hadn't learned yet that houses are still made of candy & college is
a trail of breadcrumbs gobbled up before you can make it back.
                We didn't see the trap.

The man we'd bought the house from had a new wife. She'd wanted a
fresh start. He'd bought the house with his ex-wife. They wanted a new
place to make memories without the specter of her.

It was at least two—rental—houses later & I'd jumped states again,
following those breadcrumbs when the divorce happened. When my
sister nodded through tears in the U-Haul & managed to get out,
                                "I'm not really surprised, but it still hurts."
Because lack of surprise, by itself, changes nothing about everything
else you feel. It just sort of smirks at it while all else rages on.

But most of all, I think of when Dad realized that I knew first.
                                        "Why didn't you tell me?"
Breaking down so completely I feel that I should not tell you.
                                "I couldn't."
& adult-size me
scrambling to hug him and trying to climb into his lap.
                        Of stopping just short
of punching the fuck out of my steering wheel on the highway in the
dark.

Even at probably 90 miles an hour, the most worn-out white dashes are
brighter than breadcrumbs.

It's been 20 years since that For Sale house with the broken driveway.

Dad bought me a black T-shirt with a sport's team logo: Storm.
The exact kind he would've taken from me & destroyed when I was in
high school. He called me, excited to see if I liked it.

                                        He still can't speak my name.

With all the thousands of miles we've both driven now, to make it
work:
       When we're in the car together he drives. I'm still the baby rocked to
sleep by the car seat.

It's a lifelong journey:
              building a self you can like
              letting those you love grow up.

An Apple as Apology

Melanie Hyo-In Han

// parents who show tough love // dismissing mental health //
// demanding tiger moms // workaholic dads // obsessed with wealth //

// absence // fat-shaming // racial slurs // hate //
// lashing out with thrown objects // yelling irate //

// strict moms and dads // unrealistic goals // harsh critique //
// emotionally distant // unsupportive // abusive // quick to speak //

// their words "I love you" and "I'm sorry" never spoken //
// a love that remains unexpressed // even though unbroken //

and sometimes they
bring us carefully
cored perfectly
peeled apple slices
that look like smiles

is it a coincidence that
the korean word
사과
is both the word for
"apple"
and "apology"
?

Chartreuse is shaped like red
Bethany Tap

when I was a kid, I gave everyone a color:
mom yellow, sister purple, best friend orange,
and my dad was red, folded and flowing like
an unraveling tragedy, spilling out
half-formed, half-there, half-despair,
half-rage, and smelling scarlet like cinnamon,
like a toilet seat left up, pee on the edge, acrid
in my nostrils, like a fogged exhale, the bright pinch of
a cigarette flare against black night and stars.

Of course, I was green, as my dad might say,
sharp as fresh-cut grass, hard as the rock hiding
under moss blankets, a flowing color, too,
shaped like waves one moment,
algae-studded pond the next,
red's hope, antithesis, and counterpoint.

On my 21st birthday, my dad bought me a beer,
and I bummed him a cigarette, the tips
glowing green as we breathed.
Seafoam, shamrock, sage, chartreuse
unfurled, filling the air like a swan song,
a farewell to youth, an embracing
of my birthright: to run ragged red
until every color quiets to gray.

回家

LuLu Grant

I am 29 years old the first time I see a photo of you. I fixate on your face. Those eyebrows. Those eyes. That nose. That mouth. All shocking because although I have never imagined what you look like, I never dreamed I would look like you. But I do. I can't pinpoint what, but some part of you looks like some part of me. It's a thrill because I've never matched with anyone before. Not my green and blue-eyed parents who adopted me. Not my adopted sister who, although Chinese like me, resembles no part of me. And definitely not Lucy Liu or Jackie Chan, the only famous Chinese people I knew as a kid. My heart is swelling with joy when it hits me: this is the face of the man who abandoned me. I plunge into grief.

I've known about you for as long as I can remember. Growing up, my parents called you my Chinese papa. "He loved you so much," they said, trying to soften the blow. They used language a five-year-old could understand, oversimplifying China's severe poverty, traditional patriarchal culture, and one-child policy—all contributing to why you left me on the street as a newborn. I understood one thing. You left me.

****

The first words you write me: 女儿我真的好想你了.

My eyes scan the characters in disbelief. You call me daughter. You tell me how much you have missed me. I crumble into tears. You called me daughter. You told me you really missed me. That means you never forgot me.

I wish I could reciprocate. I wish I could call you Baba, but I can't because although, yes, you are my birth father, you are a stranger. I wish I could tell you how much I've missed you, but I don't think I have, at least not recently. When I was a child, I whispered to you across an ocean. I shared mundane tidbits about my life. Sometimes, I asked you questions. *What are you doing*? *Are you happy*? *Are you alive*? Those nights, tears pooled in my ears and spilled onto my pillow as I waited for an answer I knew would never come. Does that mean I missed you? And then there was that day in fifth grade when my PE teacher selected me to participate in a free-throw contest. Me, a skinny, short Chinese girl who wasn't on a basketball team but could swish like one who was. When I told Papa after school, he chuckled and said, "Maybe someone in your family is athletic." He didn't mean our family, the one created through adoption, but yours. I liked this idea, thinking I had this athleticism, this hand-eye coordination, because someone biologically related to me could. Finally, a connection. But eventually I grew up. I stopped talking to you. I stopped imagining you shooting hoops. I did my best to forget you. It was easier, less confusing, and less painful that way.

The first words I write to you are in English: *I am so happy we found each other. I can't believe it.*

****

We are restless. You in China. Me in Mexico. For a month, we wake throughout the night and instinctively grab for our phones, our only means of connecting, the only way to quell our racing hearts and minds. We write.

You tell me you didn't go to school, that you can't do heavy work because you used to be sick, that you had surgery. I want details, but you only tell me you are okay now. I hope that is true because losing you when I just found you would be unbearable. You tell me about your mother who died when you were 20, your father who died when you were 40, and your six siblings—three of which are dead, one by suicide. So much pain. You tell me about Mother and my three siblings. Brother who is about to get married. Older Sister who works in a light bulb factory. Younger Sister who is a Chinese teacher. They are the children you kept. You tell me about your friend who found his long-lost daughter after he submitted his DNA to the police, how you did the same, and 10 days later, received the call that there was a match in the national database. You tell me your heart was thumping, that you were so excited you couldn't sleep for days. You tell me you prefer dogs to cats, that you like to exercise, especially dancing. You tell me a lot, but it's not enough.

I tell you I grew up riding horses, playing volleyball, and practicing piano. I tell you I went to college and became a nurse, that I moved to Mexico and started teaching English. I tell you I am married, that my husband is a good man and no, we don't have a baby, but a dog. I tell you about my trip to China three years ago and how I searched for you. About publishing my story online, meeting with reporters, giving a blood sample to a famous police investigator, and participating in an interview that almost aired on the local news you would have seen. I don't tell you I roamed the streets, parks, and malls of our hometown, staring at faces hoping to see one that mirrored mine.

I ask you a question in Chinese: 你会打篮球吗? *Can you play basketball*?

不会, you answer.

I laugh because you can't. I would have laughed if you could. I ask you an important question: 为什么? *Why*?

You tell me because you were so poor. That you had to save Older Sister who had fallen from three floors and cracked her head open. You tell me you wrapped me in a blanket, placed me in a bamboo basket, and before the sun rose, left me by the orphanage gate. I was 12 hours old. You tell me you are so sorry and ask for my forgiveness. I tell you I understand, even though my heart sometimes doesn't.

我哭了吗? I ask. *Did I cry*?

不.

My heart breaks, and I wonder, if I had, would you have gone back for me?

****

Two years later, I journey 8,500 miles to meet you. It takes two days and two planes. When you see me at the airport, you rush to me. You collide into my arms. Your cautious hands caress my hair, cradle my head, and gently pat, pat, pat, my back, ensuring I am real. When you push me away to look at my face, yours is slicked with tears. It contorts in sorrow and guilt. I give you a smile, and you yank me back into your arms. Your black puffer coat crinkles against mine. This is our reunion.

A bright red banner hangs at the entrance of the neighborhood. 欢迎女儿回家 the white block characters read. They welcome me, your daughter, home. So do your friends, neighbors, and family—our family. Everyone lines the sides of the red felt carpet leading to your apartment. Some take photos. Some take videos. Some pop rainbow metallic confetti that settles in my hair. A group of 20 ladies twirling flowers chant *Huan yin. Huan yin*. Welcome. Welcome. I feel myself unraveling—the spotlight, the chaos, the emotion, your hand hooked under my arm. I have to mutter to myself: *Breathe. You can do this*. You lead me to the elaborate balloon archway in front of your doorway. We step through, and I am home.

****

When I look at you, I don't see the man who left me. I see you trying to make up for lost time, trying to be Baba.

You rush to fill my thermos with hot water every morning. You hiss as your fingertips burn while peeling my freshly boiled eggs. You make me sizzling fried noodles, your signature dish that everyone says is the best. I agree. You buy me a yellow orangish fruit I have never tasted and when I tell you I love it, you buy me more. You throw me a catered party to celebrate my homecoming. Red tents, plastic tables covered with red tablecloths, and a hundred red stools take over the street. You lead me around to the guests, toasting in my honor. You take me to a wedding, to the local opera theater, to the park where you teach me how to ride your electric motorbike. You take me to restaurants where you serve me the most tender pieces of meat, the best vegetables, and even though I say I'm full, you serve

54

me more. You take me shopping to buy me shoes and too many sweaters. You're constantly telling me to bundle up because you're afraid I will get sick. And when I do get sick, your face clouds in worry. You rush me to the doctor, pushing through people to ask where I can get my blood drawn, where you can buy medications. And then you get sick. You don't want to rest, but when I push you into bed and demand you stay there, you sleep. After we get better, we take a mountain hike. You follow me up the steep incline, huffing and puffing, but refusing to say you're tired because you want to keep up. At the top, we throw up peace signs and take a selfie. It's one of my favorites. So much of you looks like so much of me.

Whatever we do, you're my photographer, capturing insignificant moments that mean everything. Wherever we go, you're by my side, a protector. Whenever we are together, you never say you love me, but I know you do.

****

Five weeks later, when our time is up, we don't cry. We don't hug or say goodbye. You motion me to go on. I want to launch myself into your arms. I want to call you Baba and tell you I'll miss you, but I don't. I gather my suitcase and walk away. I get on an airplane and fly so far from you. Only when I reach the other side of the world do I send you the characters: 我好想你. I tell you I miss you because now, I know I do.

We send each other photos and video snippets. Sometimes, I get a glimpse of the street outside your apartment. It's been eight months, but my welcome home banner, now a faded red, still hangs. I ask if you will take it down.

不会, you answer.

My heart warms. 欢迎女儿回家 will remain. It is our proclamation to the world that your daughter has come home, that we have found each other.

EIGHTH OF SEPTEMBER
Carrie Aurelius Carlisle

For just

a few minutes

I'm single

no children

until

I feel the itch

of my cesarean

scar.

There's a trick with a pen I'm learning to do
Kalehua Kim

After Michael Ondaatje

I start at the head, work
my way down my body.
A full-length mirror helps.
I fill in each scar,
trace the raised white tissue
so my pen work burns
into my reflection.

Most are connected to
memories within reach:
a tetanus shot, a toaster burn,
a fight on the playground with
a sharp-nailed girl,
the raised whip of a jib sheet,
the barbs of a blackberry bush.
And of course, the one that
started it all, the one I
showed him at the reading,

> *Thank you for your admiration.*

When I begin to fill the
tiny rivers on my abdomen—
where the baby stretched me open,
where her growth demanded
more from my skin—
it becomes too much.
The negative spaces make
me appear hollow as a bird's bones,
a porous piece of coral.

I am standing naked
in front of the mirror
and I am running out of ink,
wishing that I had written
letters, filled myself with
words instead of black holes
to draw myself together.

EXHIBIT OF WOMEN AND AWE

Sini Marcks

I love the way museums are good at casting light and shadows
upon things that say DO NOT TOUCH. Sometimes I wish I
could get that tattooed on my body. As a woman I have grown to
hate the way my body moves through space. Museums are also
good at encasing bodies, whether through oil paintings or marble
blocks, scrolls of ancient text or tombs; we value how much space
something takes up. But when it comes to people, we are allured
by how little space a body can take up.

To this day, I cannot pinpoint my obsession with thinness,
smallness, and brokenness and how all those adjectives seem to
run parallel with "woman." When I was a little girl, my family
and I visited the Museum of Natural History in Houston, Texas.
All I remember is one moment in the Hall of Paleontology. The
spotlights were sparingly and strategically placed to draw you
close to the silhouettes of evolutionary history. I don't remember
if I was holding my mother's hand when we approached a glass
case with a black backdrop. It was illuminated from above, not
the way kids at sleepovers hold flashlights under their chins to
create devilish shadows. Pinned to the blackness, in the light, was
a collection of bones. An incomplete skeleton. Scrappy and sad.

I did not think much of it until my mother leaned down
to my ear to whisper, "This is one of the first humans to walk
upright, ever." She said it with such weight that I paid attention.
"They call her Lucy, and they say she is the mother of mankind."
My mother's eyes were filled with a type of awe I had never seen
before. And then a desire I had never known filled my chest. I
wanted someone to look at *me* like that. As if I was significant
and life changing, a discovery of the ages.

Maybe it was in seeing this sad collection of skinny fragments
I got the notion that smallness is greatness. Brokenness is
beautiful. It gives you access to a type of concentrated love

that runs deeper than your lifetime. My pursuit of the exhibit of *my* bones began in college. Shrinking the size of my meals and walking miles and miles every day, my hunt for thinness consumed me physically and spiritually.

Unfortunately, this left me constantly cold. I went to school in a city with frigid winters. Our bathroom did not have a lock, and my roommate put a scale across from the toilet. Every morning after I peed, I stepped onto it, my own version of morning prayer. I would take scalding hot showers because I was constantly cold and because I liked the way the mirror steamed up so that I could not see my reflection. After throwing away the clumps of hair that had fallen out of my head, I would step on the scale and revel at the number dropping weekly.

I would regularly sit on the old radiator in my room in desperate attempts to warm up or cradle my roommate's space heater like a baby when she was gone. At night, I furled into myself like a fetus under layers of blankets. It was hard to sleep when I could feel my bones pressing against my skin, a pressure like a chick trying to break through an eggshell. My thighs did not touch. How small could I get? I wanted to be pinned upon blackness desperately.

Eventually I got looks from people that I thought were valuable and so made me valuable. Looks that I mistook for greatness, for love, for depth and reverence. Men in beds fumbling to put condoms on. Men who cooked me dinner. I remember one man I dated cooked aglio e olio, the spaghetti noodles slick with oil and the scent of garlic filling my kitchen. My mouth watered, but I said I had already eaten and wasn't hungry.

My doctor who was monitoring my heartbeat regularly told me it was dangerously low and weak. "People with eating disorders die from organ failure," she said. "Are you sure you won't consider telling your family?" It was one night that led me to crumble entirely. My roommate had bought artisan bagels;

they were on the counter in a plastic bag. I ate half a bagel with
fluffy cream cheese and convinced myself that I was going to die.
From a fucking bagel. I called my mother who was states and
miles away and told her everything. At that moment, I wished
that I was holding her hand; I headed home.

I finished college at home as I began my recovery, a plan my
mother and I patched together with the help of a pile of books
she bought and a local dietitian. My mother never questioned
how this happened, how I let things go this far, why I did not tell
her sooner. Most nights, we ate dinner next to each other on the
couch, watching TV to distract me from the nourishment slowly
refeeding my body. My heart would race as I ate, and I would
sweat as panic crept in. I hated that I had become a walking
cliché, an anorexic college girl. But my mother would trace her
fingers up and down my arm, something she did when I was a
little girl and could not fall asleep, reminding me that *she* made
my skin in her body, out of her flesh.

In bed at night, I no longer curled up, but spread out,
hyperconscious of the way my skin touched everything, as it filled
up, slowly but surely. I imagined the sculptors who reconstructed
fossils at museums, adding chunks of clay to me, as meat and fat
and hair to my bones. To this day, I sleep with a pillow between
my thighs to avoid feeling them against each other. Everyday,
I iron out the pathways in my brain that tell me that taking up
space is bad.

I don't know what faces my mother makes when she looks
at her dark bedroom walls and thinks of me, before she goes
to sleep, after she kisses me goodnight and says, "I love you,"
in her mother tongue of Finnish. Have you ever seen a mother
chimpanzee mourn over its dead child? Clutching and carrying
the corpse for months after its death? At the time, I didn't realize
the only case I could be displayed in, for my mother to see, would
be a casket.

Today, my heart is no longer shriveling, and I call my mother all the time to tell her how lucky I am, even though she is thousands of miles away again, this time in graduate school in her home country. I think about second chances. Every day I discover something new and something beautiful even if I have seen it a million times before. Like a man holding a bouquet of flowers on the metro or a child smiling at me from a stroller.

Now, I have one mirror in my apartment. Recovery is a long process. I turn it around to lean against and face the wall after I have used it to quickly glance at my outfit or hair. Sometimes, I catch my reflection in the doors of a passing bus or a shop window, and all it is now is a phenomenon of light waves bouncing off a surface. Even though I still have a hard time seeing myself, I can't help but notice that I now have a look of awe on my face. I have no desire to be an exhibit to be looked *at* because I am concerned with how *to* look.

Body as a river channel
Mary McAfoose

I am most beautiful seam-
less. Take off the clothes,
the dyed husks. This is no
categorized fruit shape,
an apple or pear. I see
a river barely contained;
what is a hip, if not
an undulation?
Let us not create lines
when there lies no such
rigidity, no stiffness here,
only soft curves: belly
becoming breasts,
neck flowing to shoulder.
How can this form be divided
into top and bottom, into
small and medium and no-we-
don't-carry-that-size. Look.
In the mirror I am
unbroken.

It was pleasure, and I clung to it
Jessica Zarrillo

the way cream soda foams excitedly
while sticking to my tongue; like out-
of-season, pesky pollen clinging to the
individual hairs inside my nose; like
Hell itself would unleash if even one
of my fingers slackened; like barnacles
sticky-kissing the bottom of rotten ships
that represent putrid rich-boy cartoon
villains; like convenient, meaty metaphors
disguising desperation and its first cousin
once removed, codependence; like a
frightened child; like warm sushi rice;
like incomprehensibly sore fists with
refusal built into them; like I woke up
from a lifelong dream, breathless and
violently recalling that I have so much
worth fighting for.

Unwrapping
Laura Taber

It's not a treasure hunt for a faraway prize.

It's an unwrapping—
a gag gift packaged in layers
and layers
of nested boxes.

My first molting
found me naked before the mirror,
ready to meet my truest self,
only to feel the next layer of fresh skin
itching to be sloughed off, too.

Herein lies my deepest fear:
that beneath these layers—
beneath
the stories I've collected,
the mental illness diagnoses,
the personality test results,
the roles I play,
the empty beliefs I've held—
beneath it all will be a pale, fleshy nymph,
grotesque, raw,
wriggling uncomfortably in the sudden exposure
to bright light.

Or worse: that there will be nothing,
just air;
the final tiny box so stark in its white emptiness,

all hope dissipated.

The Pool
Alyce Shu

I don't want to write poetry. I've had enough, this chia seed enema
of my metaphysical gut. Emotion scumbling the delicate lie
into cathedral windows of truth.

The more I write the more it matters, and I no longer desire
to know what my diverticula know. Which is,

      cycles of threes
        a scholar stone's lack
      ice chip relief and the way definitive knowledge
                                   frays
               like paintbrushes
                left in water

I'm ready to stop here, delve no deeper into the pools in which I have
                                  already begun
                                    to wrinkle.

I can't possibly keep breathing if I stay.

And ultimately, the pool never ends.

Suddenly, the pool is a waterfall. Suddenly the pool peers over
                                 a Roman ruin.

Sometimes, the pool lays train tracks and sees only in sepia.
Sometimes, the pool does a pull up, or at least, a dead
                                 hang.

The pool wins a prize of angelic tangerines.
The pool masturbates clay and consolidates forces.
The pool lathers in a pool of laughter.
The pool is the flake that begins the avalanche.

The pool snacks on krill. The pool kills for snacks.

The pool cannot get a word in and is used to being ignored.

The pool broke a nail when the pool sliced the pool's finger
                         a spoon through a sundae slid,
                                    the too-small knife.

The pool got the news that the pool's park was on fire.
That day, the pool lost the pool's job.
The pool does not know if the pool can be a mom.

The pool puddles at the bottom of the stargate.
                         Fiction facts in the gloom of a portal
the pool selects to subscribe to willful ignorance.

The pool wants to have already ascended to the fifth dimension.

The pool spills the pool's guts, the pool's guts spoil the pool's meal,
the pool's meal will last for weeks, the pool's weak
                    -ness is that the pool
                    uses everything in the pool's life
                    as an excuse to be
                         second best.

The pool is embarrassed to think in bests.

The pool doesn't respond. What is there to respond? A good life

> hurts like heather
> and a bad one like hail,
> the former regenerating
> after a light burn,
> the latter a surprise
> when falling
> beneath sunshine,

> the pool's wool sweater
> now filled with those frozen pellets
> like tiny thumbs
> stroking the amygdala,
> the pool a wet pelt,
> dissolving
> on a human
> timeline.

Contributors

Storm Ainsely has lived in nine of the United States and will tell you she's from fictionland. She has been writing since she learned to read and her answer to "What do you want to be when you grow up?" was always "An Author." Her work has appeared in *Wild Roof Journal*, *Oakwood*, *Trace Fossils Review*, *Exist Otherwise*, and *West Trade Review*, among others.

Heather Brown Barrett is an award-winning poet in southeastern Virginia. She mothers her young son and contemplates life, the universe, and everything with her writer husband. She is a member and regular student of The Muse Writers Center, a member of The Poetry Society of Virginia, and a former board member of Hampton Roads Writers. Her work has appeared in *Literary Mama*, *The Ekphrastic Review*, *Yellow Arrow Journal*, *Black Bough Poetry*, *OyeDrum Magazine*, and elsewhere. She's the author of *Water in Every Room* (Kelsay Books, 2025). Find her at heatherbrownbarrett.com.

Michelle Bovée Stange is an emerging writer exploring creative forms after over a decade in the research and journalism space. At present she is a digital nomad with her husband, son, and little black cat. Find her on BlueSky @itsmagicalmcb.bsky.social.

Kellie D. Brown is a violinist, conductor, music educator, poet, and award-winning writer of the book *The Sound of Hope: Music as Solace, Resistance and Salvation During the Holocaust and World War II*. Her words have appeared in *The Galway Review*, *Earth & Altar*, *Amethyst Review*, *Psaltery & Lyre*, *Still*, *The Primer*, *Writerly*, and others.

Tricia Gates Brown's poetry has appeared in *ANTAE Literary Magazine*, *Dorothy Parker's Ashes*, and *Friends Journal*, among other publications; her debut novel *Wren* won a 2022 Independent Publishers Award Bronze Medal. By trade, she is an editor and cowriter, mainly working for the National Park Service and Native tribes. Her first poetry collection is forthcoming from Fernwood Press mid-2025. For fun, she makes art. She resides on a farm in Willamette Valley, Oregon.

Carrie Aurelius Carlisle is a writer who'll say, her ancestral heart is German, and she's been here before. She wrote her first poem at the age of nine and hasn't put down her pen yet. She writes with brevity and strength that will fascinate all who read her.

Brandy Bell Carter is a high school English teacher in Wake Forest, North Carolina, and lives nearby with her husband. She is inspired by the beauty of nature, bluegrass, Mary Oliver's poems, and the Psalms. Her work has been published in *The Wake Forest Review* and *Y2K Quarterly*.

Alexis F. is a Southern poet of womanist flair. Originally from Virginia, Alexis traces her maternal roots across the Gullah-Geechie shorelines of South Carolina. Alexis is a graduate of the College of William and Mary and North Carolina Central University School of Law. Her work aims to center the displaced, the marginalized, and the wanderers.

Hillary Gonzalez (she/they) is a queer, genderfluid, disabled, and autistic poet whose work explores themes of nature, identity, and healing. Growing up on a farm in rural Virginia, in the foothills of the Blue Ridge Mountains, it was there where Hillary's love of nature was kindled. Their debut self-published collection, *Seasons*, quickly grew a following on Instagram, resonating with readers through its honest exploration of love, grief, growing up in an abusive home, and resilience. Hillary now lives in Baltimore, Maryland, where they continue to connect with readers on the intersections of neurodivergence, queerness, and environmental advocacy. Hillary has a collection of ecopoetry coming in 2026 with Gnashing Teeth Publishing.

LuLu Grant is a transracial, international Chinese adoptee writer. She currently lives in Mexico where she teaches ESL to children online around the world. She has words in *Hippocampus Magazine* and *Glassworks Magazine*. She is working on a memoir.

Melanie Hyo-In Han, born in Korea and raised in East Africa, recently moved from the United States to the United Kingdom. She is the author of *Abecedarian: Banff, Canada* (kith books), *My Dear Yeast* (Milk & Cake Press), and *Sandpaper Tongue, Parchment Lips* (Finishing Line Press), as well as the translator of several collections of Spanish poetry (Hebel Ediciones). She has been awarded fellowships from Gladstone's Library, The Society of Authors, Sundress Academy, Banff Centre, and Casa Uno. She is Coeditor-in-Chief of Flora Fiction and Two Languages Prize Editor at Gasher Press. Learn more about her at melaniehan.com.

Kalehua Kim is a Native Hawaiian poet living in the Pacific Northwest. Her poems have appeared in *Poetry Northwest*, *Denver Quarterly*, and *'Ōiwi, A Native Hawaiian Journal*. Her first poetry collection, *Mele*, is forthcoming from Trio House Press in July 2025.

Majiq Vu Mai (they/we) is a multiplicity of madness, writing themselves alive with the words they have access to and the words they do not know yet. An alchemist of flesh and memory, Majiq writes whatever burns inside of them like a searing ache and finds relief in giving voice to the truths that no one else wants to hear. For Majiq, memoir is a form of self-constructed fiction—we write to recollect the pieces of ourselves we have lost along the way and remember our possibilities through the creative act of storytelling.

Mansi is a writer and creativity facilitator exploring themes of identity, human connection, and the ripple effects of kindness. Her work examines the complexities of motherhood, cultural boundaries, and personal transformation. She is currently writing a book on the intersection of art, storytelling, and everyday generosity, forthcoming from Schiffer Craft in spring 2026. Through her work, she encourages others to embrace creativity as an act of self-trust and presence. She lives in California with her family.

Sini Marcks is from Austin, Texas, and received her BA in English (creative writing) from the University of Wisconsin-Madison. She currently lives in Helsinki, Finland.

Mary McAfoose (she/her) lives and works in Seattle, Washington, on the unceded ancestral lands of the Coast Salish people. She holds a degree in electrical engineering, and when not working corporate tech jobs, she enjoys writing relatable poetry, reading, and playing video games.

Shannon McNicholas is a social worker in West Virginia. California-born, Shannon decided to settle in the hills of Appalachia. In her free time, she enjoys hiking, gardening, cooking, and writing. She lives with her partner and cat in Morgantown.

Nia P. is a writer from Atlanta, Georgia, with a love for poetry and fiction. She has been published in *The Whimsical Press*, *Moss Puppy Magazine*, *Livina Press*, *Poetry as Promised*, and a few more. She has her master's in library and information science, hoping to spend her days surrounded by books and art while writing about love and magic. Find her on Twitter @NiapLuna.

Emma Reyes (she/her) is a queer Cuban poet from Miami, Florida. She earned her MFA at Florida State University this past summer. Her work has been published in *Five South Review*, *Wussy*, and *Leavings Literary Magazine*.

Lindsay B. Sears (she/her) writes as a way to practice attentiveness. Good days always include birdsong and times of discovery with her human and feline companions. She has contributed to *Still Point Arts Quarterly*, *Green Ink Poetry*, *Willawaw Journal*, and *The Shallott*. She has worked as a high school science teacher and mental health nurse. She is currently a graduate student in liberal arts at Auburn University in Montgomery, Alabama.

Alyce Shu is the daughter of Chinese immigrant doctors and a Pan-New Yorker who studied international relations and history at the University of St. Andrews in Scotland. She coorganizes the monthly City Reading Series at P&T Knitwear and has read her work at Brooklyn Poets, Bowery Poetry Club, and the Brooklyn Poetry Slam. After a decade as a creative mercenary in the entertainment and tech industries, she is currently pursuing her MFA in poetry at the City College of New York.

Cat Speranzini is Editor-in-Chief of Grey Coven Publishing, a mother, a reader for Querencia Press, and an Emerson College alumni. Her third poetry collection, *Of Verbena and Vitriol*, is pending publication with Octave Eight Publishing. So far, her work has appeared in 10 publications, including *The Eunoia Review*, *Moss Puppy Magazine*, *Clever Fox Lit*, and Glass Gates Publishing. She was recently longlisted for the Black Fox Lit contest Portraits of Failure. Find her on Instagram @thepoeticfeline.

Sara J. Streeter (she/her), or 한혜숙 Hea Sook Han, is a writer and a Korean-American adoptee. Since starting her writing journey in 2021, Sara found her writing community through Adoptee Voices and developed a meaningful connection to readers, both within the adoption constellation and beyond. She mainly writes creative nonfiction prose and has been published in literary journals, such as *Longleaf Review*, *Hippocampus Magazine*, *Peatsmoke Journal*, *The Rappahannock Review*, *GASHER Journal*, *Cutleaf Journal*, and others. She has a short story forthcoming in *An Anthology of Rural Stories by Writers of Color* (EastOver Press, 2025). Sara has been nominated for Best of the Net, Best Microfiction, and Best Small Fiction. She lives in Silver Spring, Maryland, with her family and is an interior designer for a small hospitality firm. Find her at sarajstreeter.com.

Beverley Sylvester is a writer, dramaturg, composer, musician, and visual artist. Much of her work is rooted in the southern gothic genre—combining history and research with the macabre, grotesque, and unsettling—and often centers themes of womanhood, sexuality and gender, religion, and nature. Her writing has been recognized through the Artistine Mann Award in Playwriting, the New South Young Playwrights Award, and acceptance into the Juniper Writing Institute for poetry. She graduated from Emory University and currently works at Georgia Tech.

Laura Taber is a mom of two who was born, raised, and currently resides in Baltimore, Maryland. She has a BS from Vanderbilt University and works in marketing for retail and tech brands. She enjoys journaling, drawing, hiking, exploring Baltimore, and spending time with her family. She was published in the 2024 Yellow Arrow Vignette AMPLIFY. Through her writing, Laura aspires to capture and share a raw and honest view of the human experience.

Bethany Tap is a queer writer, wife, and mom of four. Her poems and stories have been published in *Litmosphere, Fahmidan Journal, Emerge Literary Journal, Yellow Arrow Journal, Anodyne Magazine,* and *The MacGuffin,* among others. Her debut novel, *Upon the Burning,* is forthcoming in 2025 with Midnight Meadow Publishing. Find more of her work at bethanytap.com.

Jo Tyler is a queer poet, storyteller, and visual artist. A former Penn State professor and Fortune 500 VP, in retirement she returned to poetry after decades of business and academic prose. Her poems have been published in *Maryland Literary Review* and *MacQueen's Quinterly.* Delighted to be building a community of creative writers, she holds an abiding belief in the power of small groups to accomplish great things, from achieving social justice in organizations to workshopping a poem that just isn't quite there yet. Jo lives in Baltimore, Maryland, with her wife Gail and her dog Moxie.

Jessica Zarrillo is a writer and artist living in New York. She earned her bachelor's from Rutgers University in philosophy, communications, and psychology. By day, she works in marketing; by night, she plays video games and laments. Her work can be found in *Starcrossed Poetry Community: Anthology I,* among a number of other zines and publications. Find her online at jesszarr.com or on social media @SourNothings.